I SEE YOU
BROTHA

This book comes off the back of a mental breakdown. I'd felt like I failed and was failing at everything I attempted or was trying to accomplish. No matter how much I pushed, nothing was budging; my efforts didn't feel like enough; it always required more. I have done enough work on myself to realize when I need to reach out to someone or get on my knees and pray for clarity of why I feel a certain way. What is it that's bothering me, what decisions have I made that were rushed? Why am I not being grateful? Through prayer, the answer came to me that in this time of feeling low, it is in this moment you need to speak for others as well. I realize I am not the only one who felt my feelings that day.

This work is dedicated to my son Lyric and to all my brothas.

Although stories may differ, we fight the same fight.

In a world that makes you feel unwanted and undeserving

I want you to realize you are deserving from the hard work you do

So, my brothas, this is for us

And to those who love us, care for us, adopt us, or mentor us;

Continue to learn us, understand us, care, and continue giving us the

space to learn, care, and love ourselves.

1 Corinthians 15:28

Therefore, my beloved brothers, be steadfast,

immovable, always abounding in the work of the Lord,

knowing that in the Lord, your labor is not in vain.

(KJV) James 1:1-27

TABLE OF
CONTENTS

Acknowledgment ix

It's Just Me 1

This vs. That (Finding true happiness) 3

Society's typical black males 9

The Adam Effect 21

Due Season 23

Sticking Point 25

Growth in struggle 29

Checkmate 39

Mind-Body Connection 45

Sins of the Father 51

Intergenerational Trauma 55

A Missed Dream.. 57

Why Would We Want Our Children to Go Through That?.................. 61

Creating Program/Community... 67

Tap In 71

ACKNOWLEDGMENT

Within the last few years, black men's mental health, thankfully, is a topic of discussion. In recent years, the number of male suicides has continued to climb due in part to the belief that no one knows or cares to understand the plight of being a black man. In an article printed in 2023 by ABC Action News, according to the suicide prevention resource center, "Young African American men commit suicide at more than three times the rate of African American women. The suicide rate for black children ages 10-19 has risen 60% just over the past two decades, outpacing any other racial or ethnic group."

The dynamic of suffering in silence in fear of being viewed as weak has to change. Bishop TD Jakes speaks on being disruptive in his book Disruptive Thinking. Being a disruptive thinker, you do not sit and continue living in a world that doesn't afford you opportunities and complain about it. A disruptive thinker shakes things up and makes things happen. Changing the narrative of what a man and father are examples of disrupting societal norms of telling you what you are, who you should be, and what you are not doing.

Before we dive into this book, I believe it is essential to acknowledge and celebrate those who put forth their best foot for the betterment of themselves and others. Dr. Jay Barnett and Jeremy Wright are two gentlemen who, in my opinion, are taking charge of improving black men's image, health, and well-being and placing them at the forefront. In Disruptive Thinking, Bishop Jakes describes what a disruptive thinker is and does. He says, "Disruptors don't take sides, they take over." We can sit back and continue letting people tell us who we are and what we are supposed to do, or we can flip the narrative on its head and make it what we want to be known for. In my opinion, Brothas like Jay Barnett and Jeremy D. Wright are examples of disruptive thinkers.

Jeremy D. Wright is a dedicated community servant who prides himself in loving people, inspiring others, and driving positive change through community activism. After graduating with a Bachelor of Science in Psychology from Fayetteville State University, he furthered his academic endeavors by pursuing a Master of Divinity degree at United Theological Seminary. Jeremy has left a footprint in multiple sectors, including the mental health field, entertainment management, and publishing. He is the founder and Executive Director of AsOne Fellowship., a non-profit organization that fosters reconciliation and community unification through various activities and services. He is strongly dedicated to uplifting and empowering the black community, which led him to start BrotherStrong.

BrotherStrong is built on personal proclamation, individual responsibility, and collective accountability. Its motto, "I am, You are, We are… BrotherStrong!" reflects the spirit of unity and strength that Jeremy strives to nurture within the black Community. Along with all his accomplishments and accolades, Jeremy is also an accomplished author. With his published works: "Love Letter to My Son: Navigating Love without the Proper Example from Me" and "TO ALL THE GIRLS I LOVED BEFORE GOD," he continues to highlight where we as black men were, where we are, and where we can go as individuals and as a collective.

Dr. Jay Barnett is a former professor athlete who found struggle in life after sports. Through surviving the dark encounters, he made it through to the other side, realizing that God had called him to more than he could even imagine. He came to understand that his tests made room for his testimony, which he uses to inspire and encourage those who may be going through or have gone through some of the same encounters. As a pastor's son, he understands having roots in the spiritual and the feeling of being neglected and left behind. Those feelings are the feelings and reality of so many of us as black men. Dr. Barnett said, "Society and schools have left us behind, and so many other impactful areas of our lives have been set up to prevent us from progressing in life. I am blessed and honored to be able to be in a place to help men find themselves and also challenge themselves to grow spiritually, mentally, emotionally, and physically.

Society doesn't give us the room to pause and catch our breath, so I wanted to provide a place to stop and be. I want to build our men and not have them having to navigate life on their own". Dr. Barnett is an accomplished therapist, speaker, and author with works like Hello King and JUST HEAL BRO; he shows that there is strength in vulnerability, there is no need to hold on to the very thing that is killing us, and there is strength in community. You deserve an opportunity to rest and just be. JUST HEAL BRO is a book designed to help black men find strength in vulnerability as well as mental and emotional healing through education and community, and is doing the groundwork to disrupt the narrative of men being unable to express and articulate their feelings intelligently. He shares the narrative that men are human and thus have feelings. Yes, we must be strong, but we also must be able to have the space necessary to feel safe enough to unload the feelings that can turn into anger, stress, and depression.

These are the examples of BLACK MEN that society chooses to make known. They are prime examples of disruptive thinkers trying to change what is portrayed by changing the narrative. Brothas like Jeremy D. Wright and Dr. Jay Barnett make what I am trying to do worth it. We have a voice, and it should be heard!

Philippians 4:12

I know how to be brought low, and I know how to

abound. In any and every circumstance, I have

learned the secret of facing plenty and hunger,

abundance and need

IT'S JUST ME

Before we dive into Brotha, I See You, I'd briefly like to take a step from behind the curtain. My name is David Brunson. I am the third born of five children, so if you just thought about middle child syndrome, you hit the nail right on the head.

Depression and the feeling of neglect or being undesired were a regular thing for me. By the time I was 10, I tried killing myself twice. The sad part is that 2024 was the first time my parents knew about it. I moved around quite a bit, having gone to 16 schools before going to college. I found the church and the football field to be relief places because I could relate the most.

Football became something more than life to me to the point that when I no longer had it, I lost all sense of my identity. Not having the thing I most wanted and felt safe in, I once again found myself in a position of wanting to take my life. It took almost six years before I finally got myself together. It took that long because I didn't allow anyone to help me. It took a lot of prayer to find my reason for being here and writing this book.

I am here today because I know I have a purpose. I realize I have my son who is looking at me to guide him through this crazy game called life. Having gone through so much early in my life, I refuse to have him go through the same things. I may not be able to leave him a bunch of riches, but if there is something I will leave him, it is how to make better decisions than I did, how to make more than I did, and whatever knowledge I gained through this tumultuous life I've lived; he will have. From heartbreak and heartache, wrong place wrong time, understanding who you are, and not finding yourself through the eyes of others. The list could go on and on.

My faith plays a huge role in my life, so throughout the book, you will find scriptures that relate to the discussed topics. I believe the bible speaks to many of the very issues being discussed in everyday life today, just in different terms. I ask that you not shut your mind off because it is a bible verse; instead, understand what I am saying. I can only say what has been given to me and how to say it. You could very well get something entirely different once you read it.

THIS VS. THAT
(FINDING TRUE HAPPINESS)

It is easy to fall into the trap of what you have is not enough. This idea has ruined the mental state of so many, and they don't even know what's happened. I've realized that most people don't understand the differences between contentment vs satisfaction and gratitude vs gratification.

- Contentment, although having a slight sense of satisfaction, is one of peace and ease of mind. It is being grateful for what you have or where you are.

- Satisfaction is the fulfillment of one's wishes, expectations, needs, or pleasures.

Two other words similar in context or meaning are gratitude and gratification.

- Gratification is the fleeting thrill of receiving.

- Gratitude is being appreciative

The Bible speaks of these things as being either building or destructive characteristics.

From the beginning of time, we see battling with gratification or satisfaction. In the book of Genesis (we all should know the story of Adam and Eve by now), God gave Adam his role and placed him over everything, including his woman, Eve. No, to be over doesn't mean to be boisterous or belittling but to have everything under your care. He was responsible for ensuring she lived by the same laws God gave Adam. Eve was tricked into eating from the Tree of Knowledge of Good and Evil, which God said not to eat from, and Adam followed. The desire for more money, women, food, etc, has negatively impacted many lives. It isn't just the desires; being tricked into believing what you have is insufficient. There's a saying, "If you once prayed for what you have now, if you once hoped to be where you are right now, then you are living your dream." Contentment and gratitude do not mean you've settled; it just means you are thankful for what you have; it doesn't mean you will not grow into something more; it is just placing more in its proper place.

Some believe that psychology doesn't have a place in religion but, when you look at it a little closer, everything about the bible has a psychological aspect to bettering one's mind, body, and soul in dealing with matters of the heart, mind, and spirit. I grew up in the church and have dealt with a lot in my life, so I know the power of prayer but also believe in seeking wise counsel. Not only does the bible speak on counsel, but it also gets into the mind-body connection.

One's heart and mind are connected and can affect the health of your body.

> "Blessed is the man who walks not in the counsel of the wicked, nor stands in the way of sinners, nor sits in the seat of scoffers, but his delight is in the law of the Lord, and in his law he meditates day and night. He is like a tree planted by the stand of water that yields its fruit in its season, and its leaf does not wither. In all that he does, he prospers."
>
> ~Psalms: 1:1-3~

"A sound heart is the life to the body, but envy is rottenness to the bones" Proverbs 14: 30 In other versions, it would read, "A sound mind makes for a robust body, but runaway emotions corrode the bones"

Your happiness is not tied to what you acquire (d), but where you place its importance. You will always be unhappy if chasing money is your goal. There will always be more printed, there will always be more women than you will ever see, and there will always be more food until there isn't. I'm not saying there will never physically be more, but placing

5

them in their proper places will allow you to see where your true happiness and blessings are.

You are more than what you have, where you are, how much money you make, the car you drive, how many women you can get, or the house you live in. When ambition grows beyond your contentment, happiness will be an illusion tied to possessions.

> "Be on your guard against all kinds of greed for a man's life does not consist in the abundance of his possessions."
>
> Luke 12:15

We are responsible for creating our happiness, so let us start by addressing some underlying issues that could block one's view of how to get there.

Step outside of the box. People create those boxes for their comfort

> This world will tell you that you're angry, but has anyone ever tried to figure out why that is the case?

> How often have you been asked how you are doing, and the person truly meant it?

> Have you heard the words I love you, appreciate you, am proud of you, or see you?

Have you been able to show emotion without being judged or having it thrown back in your face?

If you're anything like me, your answer would be never or no.

So many questions need to be asked about why we are perceived as angry. Is that perception even fair or accurate?

> YOU DESERVE THE OPPORTUNITY TO CREATE YOUR STORY AND LIVE A LIFE NOT BOUND BY OTHER'S PERCEPTIONS OF WHO YOU ARE OR SUPPOSED TO BE IN THEIR EYE

SOCIETY'S TYPICAL
BLACK MALES

In a place that constantly labels us angry and violent, lazy, criminals, dead beats, broken, unstable, not needed, the bottom of the barrel, and the list goes on, the one thing they will refuse to see is our resilience. No matter what we are given, we still find a way to make something happen. It may differ in how desired or digestible it is, but it gets done. You still find a way to make it happen, even in a world that constantly turns you away because of your hair, underqualified, overqualified (whatever that means), or even your skin color. This preconceived notion that you are not deserving says nothing about who you are.

To understand where anger comes from, it's essential to break down these stereotypes that can potentially hold one back in growth, whether financial, mental, educational or even familial.

Stereotypes and stigmas about black men and young black boys have been prevalent in America for many years. It's important to acknowledge that these stereotypes can perpetuate biases and misconceptions and do not represent the majority of black men, leading to discrimination and unequal treatment. Are there bad apples? Of course, you can say that about anything or any group of people. Negative social views can have significant consequences, leading to disparities in education, employment, criminal justice, and healthcare. Black boys may face disproportionate disciplinary actions in school, limited access to quality education and resources, and increased interactions with law enforcement due to racial profiling.

I've been in many places and situations where I walked into people automatically labeling me with the very stereotypes. In two different situations and places, I found myself in predominantly white schools, one in Ponte Vedra, FL, and the other in Cedar City, Utah. In both places, you could feel the differences. Still, it was primarily in Utah that I would meet other races that had never had an interaction with a black person before. Hence, the only thing they could base the knowledge of black Americans on was what they saw on television or what someone would tell them. If you ask for information from the wrong people, you'll most likely carry on that information if you don't research it or gain experience. I would be treated as if I was only there because of football, but little did they know that my grades could get me into better schools than that one. Those views would continue until they saw what they thought was not the same thing they had been told or shown their entire lives. From sitting on panels at the school to playing football, I was looked at differently until they learned about myself and the other black student-athletes to form their own opinions. Of course, you'll never be able to change everyone's minds, but be who you are; they'll think whatever they want anyway.

Diving into some of these stereotypes:

Criminality:

One of the most pervasive stereotypes is the assumption that black males are more likely to partake in criminal behavior. This is a stereotype often fueled by media portrayals, which can and oftentimes lead to racial profiling, unfair treatment by law enforcement, and systemic biases in the criminal system. According to the U.S. Sentencing Commission, black males received sentences 20.4 percent longer than their white counterparts. In various states, those numbers could be much higher. That is a conversation for another day.

Drug use/ Dealing:

There's a running theory that black males are disproportionately associated with drug use and dealing, which in turn fuels the perception that they are inherently involved in criminal activities. The ideology is followed by racial biases and unfair targeting by law enforcement, but it also ignores the vast majority of law-abiding black males and also ignores the root of the problem.

Violent and aggressive:

There's been a picture painted of black males that portrays us as inherently violent and aggressive. This stereotype has overlooked that an individual's behavior is influenced by various factors such as upbringing, environment, personal choices, and services available to them to help rather than being determined by the color of their skin. Additionally, there's the stereotype of being thugs and/or being associated with gang activity and criminal behavior.

Hypermasculinity:

Black males are often depicted as hypermasculine, reinforcing stereotypes that we are overly aggressive, dominant, and lacking emotional vulnerability. This one takes a toll negatively on mental health, and it perpetuates harmful expectations of masculinity.

I'm inclined to believe that societal views on not only what a man is but being a black man have created a lot of resentment and anger in many of us, and without a proper way of letting it out, could present itself in many ways. I do not believe that we are "hyper-masculine," but we are misunderstood and borderline being forced into the characteristics described.

Hypersexualization:

This is a conversation that when someone hears hypersexualizing, they associate only with women when, in fact, this is a topic that affects black men as well. Black males have historically been hypersexualized, perpetuating stereotypes that are excessively sexual and predatory. Just like one would say for women, it objectifies and contributes to the dehumanization and mistreatment of black males.

I believe this topic has been worn almost as a badge of honor due to subscribing to the conversations around it, which often feeds our ego but builds an unrealistic view of what makes us who we are. I think many of us have the same story of having adult women (teachers, friends of parents, babysitters, etc) have either verbally said something or acted on whatever fantasy they had in their minds. Early on, we might've looked at it as something to brag about, but in the long term, it created something of a skewed outlook on sexuality.

Intellectual inferiority:

This stereotype has been associated with black men due to the assumption that we are intellectually inferior or less capable academically. This ignores the countless achievements and contributions made by black males in various fields perpetuate the systemic barriers we face in accessing quality education.

This conversation has various views. Some of us have gotten better opportunities than others. Some got their education from their talents in sports, others excelled in the classroom, and some could do both; with that being said, to be still viewed as inferior is a massive slap in the face. Just a few years ago, the NFL got rid of race-norming, which assumed black players had a lower cognitive function. How could such a professional organization hold negative views of those making millions? It does not only tie into the world of sports but many others. The idea of intellectual inferiority of black males continues into the socioeconomic arena as well.

Absentee fatherhood:

Black males have often carried the label of absent and have been stigmatized as lacking in responsibility when it comes to family and parenting. The stereotype overlooks the different experiences and involvement of black males in the families and perpetuates harmful stereotypes about the commitment black men have to their children.

Socioeconomic status:

The black experience shows that black males are often associated with having a low socioeconomic status, in turn, wrongfully saying we are attached to low income, unemployment, and poverty. While some experience these circumstances, it is essential to recognize that various factors influence socioeconomic status.

It has been shown that educated black men have a lower chance of getting employment than white males with a felony background. The struggle does not lay with the willingness to work but the opportunity given to and in what field. So, if the world says to get an education to improve your chances of making a better life for yourself and your family, does it stand to say those without an education don't stand a chance?

Athleticism:

While this is a positive attribute, it often puts black males in a box with the stereotype that black males are primarily valued for their athletic abilities. This view usually overlooks the many talents and achievements black males have been known for outside sports. This notion that black males are only successful in physical endeavors rather than recognizing who they are and what they achieve in other areas is unreasonably unfair.

Additionally, it is essential to recognize the intersectionality of these stereotypes and acknowledge that black males may also experience the compounding effects of racism and biases due to their gender. Black males may face unique challenges and discrimination that are influenced both by their race and gender identities. It is crucial to address and challenge these intersecting stereotypes and stigmas to promote equality and create a society that values and celebrates the diversity of black males and their experiences.

"A lie gets halfway around the world before the truth has a chance to get its pants on."

-Mark Twain-

With those stereotypes now out of the way, how have we, as black men, helped those stereotypes to grow so worldwide that it is hard to shake the negative view of us?

Or have we helped push the narrative at all?

How can we be better and give a better image to shake this negative image?

We can look around and see that our youth needs guidance. Heck, even some of our adults are in need. I truly believe the issue stems from misunderstanding what a man is and his purpose. The portrayal of a man is dramatically skewed beyond belief. As men, it should be our job to shape the minds of the younger men.

We are fathers, sons, builders, educators, counselors, coaches, etc. We can't just be coaches and educators of sports. We must do a better job of opening our men's minds and helping them tap into the unseen world. We must be better at unloading the feelings that are not benefiting us instead of harboring them and turning them into stress and anger. We must change the narrative of what "MAN" is instead of allowing society to determine what it is. No matter what society's outlook is, remembering that you are human and you will make mistakes, you will have feelings, and you will succeed is the most essential part of who you are as a man.

Continue to live, learn, grow, and most importantly, be you; there will never be another.

The goal of this book is to shift the mindset of men not only to want to be better versions of themselves for themselves but also better versions of the ones watching them. To help each black male, young or old, get to where they want to be. It's time to start releasing the things that are not benefiting us and creating healthier habits.

It is often disheartening when looking at the state of black men through the eyes of society. I see black men excelling in all aspects of life, but what is portrayed on television is one that is far from reality. With that being said, to sit here and say that we haven't played a role in the views would be a dishonest thought.

> A HEALTHY COMMUNITY CAN BE BUILT OR
> BROKEN DOWN, STARTING WITH US.

I believe we have gotten lost, misled, and confused along the way to where we are now. What is a man? There is a surface-level answer to that, but then there is one more in-depth that leans more to the biblical sense of man.

THE ADAM EFFECT

When discussing and describing the neglected role of man, I refer to it as "The Adam Effect." The Adam Effect explains the causation of when MAN is living out of order. When referring to biblical texts, Adam was told how things was to be, what to do, and what not to do. Adam allowed the woman made for and from him to get him out of his purpose due to her thirst for something not meant for her or anyone. Instead of following the direction given to him by God, he fell out of order.

"There is something worse than not having sight; it is having sight without vision."

~Helen Keller~

DUE SEASON

Life can seem like a weight room and, in some cases,
a waiting room. How does that even make sense?

The weight room is where individuals willingly go to break down their bodies to gain the results they're looking to attain. It's interesting how we can be okay with waiting for the results. We can put ourselves through the pain of breaking our bodies down to build them back up and be very consistent with it, but when it comes to waiting in life, it is a problem. The waiting room analogy is just another example of life and is basically the same as the weight room. It is going to take time to be seen. We go to doctors, interviews, and several other things and have to wait, but we do it because we can see there is an opportunity on the other side of waiting. There is an expectation or a vision.

When referring to the weight room, there is a time when you go at it hard to max out possible outcomes, but there is a point where things must slow down; otherwise, you risk improving your chances for injury and setting yourself back. An example of doing too much without adequate rest is overtraining. Overtraining can lead to a decline in performance and potential health issues. We all hit a plateau in performance somewhere in our lives. Sometimes, we plateau, which could be physical, mental, or even emotional, which could cause distress if we focus on not moving or progressing. There is a time to push through, lighten the load, and/or rest. Where are you?

STICKING POINT

Don't give up at your sticking point.

> STOP PUTTING A PERIOD WHERE
> GOD IS PUTTING A COMMA

We often put waiting in a negative light because it doesn't align with the timeline we have made for ourselves. We also confuse waiting with being STAGNANT and try rushing the wait, which becomes HASTE.

To be stagnant is to be in a state or condition marked by a lack of flow, movement, or development.

Haste is the undue eagerness to act. (acting without thinking, ex.) Rushing the process can lead to deformities or abnormalities.

In the process/wait stage, most of the work should be done. Trying to arrive at the destination without doing any work leads to nothing being learned, which can become a disaster.

Biblically, we are taught to wait on the Lord.

"Wait for the Lord; be strong. And let your heart take courage; wait for the Lord."

Psalms 27:14

"But they who wait for the Lord shall renew their strength; they shall mount up with wings like eagles; they shall run and not be weary; they shall walk and not faint."

Isaiah 40:31

"The Lord is good to those who wait for him, to the soul who seeks him."

Lamentations 3:25

The list of scriptures referencing waiting on the Lord goes on and on. The one thing that is not often elaborated on is that waiting has a shelf life. You can wait too long and miss out on your opportunity/blessing. Work is required in your waiting, which can help combat stagnation, but understanding your wait and your work will resist haste.

"Faith without works is dead."

James 2:26

I'm sure we've all heard more people speaking about manifesting. Would you believe me if I told you manifesting is only a part of the process? The same can be said for speaking life into something or someone. Manifesting without change is pointless.

Manifesting requires something to change. Speaking life into someone or something without breathing life into it, although it serves a purpose, it is only a part. Speaking life is the vision; without the breath (work), that vision will stay exactly like that: a vision. It all comes down to work and waiting.

GROWTH IN STRUGGLE

I believe there is a question that many of us
have asked God. WHY?.....

Why do I have to go through all this struggle constantly? Why is the one not right getting all I desire, and I am here fighting for the little I have?

No matter how good I am and how much I do, why do I not get any peace? When is it my turn? When will I arrive at the finish line?

I always asked God those questions until I appreciated my struggle/journey. I had to learn that struggle made room for maturity. You can not avoid change but you can choose to mature or stay the same. When speaking about goals or struggles, both are necessary. There are many sayings that are thrown around but never looked at past the surface. I bet most people didn't know you were quoting a part of the bible when you said, "Iron sharpens iron." (Psalms 27:17). We've heard it, said, and heard a multitude of other quotes about being under pressure and coming out on the other side or succumbing to it, but have you sat down to understand how your life is tied into those sayings?

It's easy to lose sight while in the struggle, especially if you haven't done the work to understand or experience life when it's not going your way.

WHY NOT YOU?

I was given a life of tests... huh? Given a life of tests? Yes, I was given a life of tests. I say this because I was blessed to be in a position to bless others with the understanding that we all aren't going to be blessed with the same thing but are blessed with something. What are you going to do with what you've been blessed with? Comparing your something to someone else's will have you diminishing what you have. I've gone through homelessness, journeying, shelters, losing a dream, and the breaking of a family, among a multitude of other situations in my life.

Optimize a little to gain more. I had to learn to use my experiences to bless lives. It may not be monetarily but with my actions and words.

God has blessed each of us with skills and talents. What have you done and/or what are you doing to maximize them?

Understand that suffering is not always a punishment but preparation...

I was always told to be humble, keep my head down, and work hard. Doing so would only result in good things. I was never told doing those things could get me looked over, told no, or even failed. If I am a good person, live right, and work hard, why wouldn't I get everything I am asking for? How could someone see that and step on it as if it were just trash? How could someone following everything he's been told have to go through so much, but those who couldn't care less about grades, spirituality, family, and maintaining a healthy lifestyle get everything I believed I deserved?

Why do I have to go to so many schools? Why do I always have to wear hand-me-downs? Why do I work so hard to get the little bit someone else didn't have to work for? Why be a good guy when it leads to being cheated on or overlooked? There were so many questions that I would bring to the Lord until I stopped asking and started paying attention to what was being said. I was talking myself out of my progress because the noise in my head overshadowed what I was meant for.

I would have given up a long time ago had it not been for the power I believe prayer holds. You may ask yourself, "How do you pray or talk to the Lord?". My answer would be, how do you talk to your friends or family? Your relationship or conversation with the Lord is just that: YOURS. It is something you don't have to be in a church to do; you don't have to go to someone for it; you don't have to be in a time of need or excess. It is something you do sitting or standing right where you are. I can honestly say that without my relationship with God or my prayer life, there is no way I'd be here writing this book.

My struggle or journey has allowed me to relate to many people on different levels. My prayer life has allowed me to make it to this point. Am I a completed project? Not, nor will I ever be. I take my lessons as blessings and struggles as a workout. I continue to push until it becomes easier for me to lift myself and continue on my road to my destination.

"You are more than a conqueror"

Romans 8:37

> KEEP GOING, BROTHA, AND YOU WILL SEE YOUR WORK SHINE ON THE OTHER SIDE OF THE STRUGGLE.

A great read I enjoyed for understanding the work required to see the fruits of your labor was HARVEST TIME; WHAT'S THAT ALL ABOUT by WM. Di'Mon Brown.

Putting this conversation in the monetary realm, according to various data platforms, most black men don't reach their peak earning years until between 35 and mid-40s. That is not to say you will not get there in that time, but it is possible, and there is a chance you could get there way before or even after. The question is, what are you doing with your time? We know the results oftentimes drive us, but realize that your value as a man is not tied solely to that. On all levels of life, not all things end with the results we seek. Pick yourself up and continue working, learning, and growing.

> YOU ARE NOT THE ONLY
> ONE GOING THROUGH THIS!
> KEEP YOUR HEAD UP AND KEEP STRIVING
> FOR YOUR GREATNESS.

Waiting but working in the process. The process will crush you, but the crushing is meant to build you. The process method may not be quick, but the outcome is intended to be there longer than you had to endure. Your path was made for you; others may be unable to go where you are called. The path to your destination will be shut, so don't return. Keep moving forward in purpose and trust the process.

If I were to give examples of 2 men who trusted the process instead of rushing it and came out on the other side in their calling, I'd quickly throw out Joseph and Moses.

Although Joseph's story is different from Moses's, the idea is the same in the sense of going through the struggle to get to the other side.

Joseph was the 11th son of Jacob. Jacob was highly fond of Joseph, which, in turn, made the brothers jealous. Through their jealousy, they sold him into slavery.

While in slavery, he was accused of trying to seduce his master's wife (who lied on him), leading to his imprisonment. He was imprisoned only to turn around and be called upon to decipher his master's dream. With his interpretation of the dream, Joseph became Governor of Egypt. He spearheaded preparing for the famine that was to come in Egypt. Joseph's brothers came to Egypt looking for help, and to their surprise, the brother that they sold into slavery became someone of importance and someone they would need to turn to. Joseph forgave his brothers and set his family up in Egypt.

> YOUR STORY ISN'T DONE BECAUSE
> YOU ARE IN A DOWN PERIOD

Moses was born to slaves, and to escape the order from Pharaoh to kill all newborn boys, his mother hid him in a basket and sent him on his way down the Nile. He was found by the daughter of the very man who ordered to have him killed. Moses was raised as Pharaoh's own. Not realizing his origins, Moses killed a taskmaster who was beating a Hebrew man. He fled to another city, where God would speak to him. He would return with an assignment from God to tell Pharaoh to set the Israelites free. To prove his authority, he showed signs by turning his staff into a snake and water into blood. Pharaoh did not listen, so God intervened with plagues, forcing Pharaoh to set Moses' people free. Moses would lead his people to the promised land.

> YOUR BEGINNINGS DO NOT DETERMINE
> YOUR OUTCOME

It isn't only about the process but understanding that you are called according to what God has instilled in you, the ability to overcome every obstacle placed in your path, skills, and idea

Elihu: "I am young in years, and you are old. Therefore I was afraid to tell you what I think. I thought age should speak, and increased years should teach wisdom. But it is a spirit in man, and the breath of the Almighty gives them understanding." David (a shepherd boy who goes on to defeat Goliath, commits adultery, and becomes King), Moses (a man with a speech impediment who leads his people out of Egypt), Samson, Saul (known for being a Christian killer), Jacob (a homeless grifter). A raven (sent out to test if there was dry land; Story of Noah), Plagues (frogs, locusts, flies, and hail {there are others}used in the story of Moses), a donkey (God allowed to speak), Whale (Jonah and the whale), and many other demonstrations throughout the Bible shows that anything and anyone can be used.

It doesn't matter who you are, where you've been, or where you are now. Each of us has a calling, purpose, a goal, and it is according to God's will that we get there. You must do your part to get there. You have everything you need already in you; you have to bring it forward.

MINDFUL
REFLECTIONS

CHECKMATE

Have you ever played chess?
If not, let me explain why I am bringing it up.

"That's a white thing". Something I heard when it came to the game of chess. It wasn't until I learned the game that I realized how much it relates to real life. When I sat down and understood the movement and purpose of every piece, I started understanding that life is like the game of chess. How you move, the pieces you choose to have around you, how you place and guide them, etc, will determine the kingdom's success.

I associate the game of chess with the game of life, whether in business, romantic relationships, or everyday life. Alone, you are limited in your approach as opposed to when you have other pieces. An impulsive or reactive king is bound to destroy his kingdom, but the wrong pieces around him may do the same. Protect yourself and your kingdom by making sure the ones around you always have the kingdom's sake in mind.

Chess is a game that has been around for a long time. It is used as a metaphor for various aspects of life. Some ways that chess relates to real life and how to use it as a learning tool are strategy and planning, decision-making, patience and perseverance, adaptability, consequences and actions, balancing offense and defense, and sacrifice. How does this relate to life exactly? Having a clear strategy or setting goals can help you navigate different obstacles that may come up. Decision-making skills are crucial when considering different options, weighing pros and cons, as well as predicting potential threats and consequences. Understanding patience requires you to think long-term and not get disheartened about specific outcomes and setbacks while also remaining focused on the goal in order to overcome challenges. Being able to adapt to constant changes is an art.

Chess is a dynamic game that constantly has pieces moving, so adapting to what is going on while applying the other aspects can help create creative solutions to the constant change. Understanding the balance between offense and defense lets you know when to take a risk and when to protect yourself. It's important to know when to be proactive and seize opportunities while also being mindful of possible risks and safeguarding your interests. Consequences of one's actions: I saved this one for last. Every move you make has a consequence, and you must consider whether the risk outweighs the reward before making a move. Making a move too late or too early can be a detrimental decision.

Understanding the game's nuances is one thing, but understanding the pieces is another. How do the pieces on the board relate to life? We've all heard this before; "be careful who you keep around you." Well, that saying applies to chess and life alike. In the game of chess there are eight pawns, two rooks, two knights, two bishops, one queen, and one king. Each piece has a specific pattern they must stay to. In theory, these pieces are the people you have in your life, "your circle." As the king, you are responsible for choosing those pieces, ensuring they are in the right position, knowing their role, and knowing when to move or stay still.

The most important piece on the board is the King, as every piece on the board on your side is under your care and guidance but is also there to protect you. The queen is the most dynamic piece on the board, and in life, it is one of the most critical pieces to choose correctly and invest in. Although any and every piece can aid in the growth of the kingdom, it is also important to know that the same can be said about losing the kingdom. Aside from the King being lost, none can do more damage than the Queen.

As a King, you are responsible for so much more than yourself. I believe everything can be a teacher if you want to learn. Understand that being a king or a leader does not absolve you from the same fate as anyone else. The same rules that other pieces on the board abide by, the King must abide by the same rules of the game. You are responsible for choosing the pieces in your life. If you don't trust them enough or believe they can do the required job, you need to look in the mirror. Why are they there? Understand that a King is or should be a SERVANT. To ensure your kingdom thrives, the King must, by all means, ensure that everyone can fulfill their parts. As a MAN, we must provide numerous things to ensure our family is good. One cannot do that by not submitting to one's family/kingdom somehow. To serve is not to be a slave. Seeking counsel from your pieces is not a sign of weakness but a way to become stronger as an individual and a unit.

An impulsive king will always run his kingdom into the ground. Learning to manage urges and emotions is a key to learning to lead. A great king also listens to counsel and differences of opinion and adjusts when needed.

If you act on every urge (impulse) or react to every action or verbal assault hurled at you, where does that put you and the others under your guidance? There is power in patience, understanding in focus, and victory in consistency.

Questions I'd consider asking myself about those I bring into my life:

Is this person positive, or do they cause unnecessary stress or chaos?

Am I valued, and is there value in having this relationship?

Are they draining, or do I feel energized around them?

How is communication between us?

How is conflict handled?

Is there support in this relationship?

Do we share the same values and/or goals?

"Life is like a game of chess. To win, you have to make a move. Knowing which move to make comes with IN-SIGHT, knowledge, and learning the lessons accumulated along the way."

We become every piece within the
game called LIFE!

~Allan Rufus~

MIND-BODY CONNECTION

—◆◇◆—

The mind-body connection is the relationship between an individual's mind, thoughts, behaviours, and emotional state and also someone's physical health. I do believe many of us have suffered so much with not understanding how one thing affects another pertaining to our body and mind. Understanding that our feelings and thoughts play a role in our physical health and our experiences, whether heartbreak or disappointment, shape our perception, mess with our emotional state, or even cause an injury, not only messing with the physical but also mental. Every one thing can affect another.

As a black man, I understand the struggle of carrying the weight of the world on my shoulders, just as you would too. Black men's mental and emotional health challenges go hand in hand with physical health outcomes. Yes, the same can be said for any race or group of people, but once you start talking about the unfair or unjust reality, you begin talking about something entirely different. Oftentimes, the outcomes of those mental and emotional issues manifest themselves as a severe health issue or premature death.

According to a study published by The University of Wisconsin back in 2013: <u>Depression in African American Men: A Review of What We Know and Where We Need to Go from Here,</u> "Based on the studies in the present review, the prevalence of MDD (MAJOR DEPRESSION DISORDER) among African American men ranges from 5-10%. Although the prevalence of MDD among African American men is lower compared with Caucasian men, African American men appear to experience higher rates of chronicity and disability". A few of the chronic illnesses, hypertension, diabetes, and heart disease, are associated with long-term stress or psychological distress.

Over the last two decades, the suicide rate among black boys and men has been on a rapid incline. According to the Centers for Disease Control and Prevention, suicide is the second leading cause of death for African Americans between the ages of 15 and 24. It is particularly prevalent among men, with a rate being 4 times that of black women.

Many of us have been exposed to things early in our lives we shouldn't have had to learn until we were older, let alone learning at all. The unfortunate part about it is that we believe that it is a must that we learn and understand these things so we know how to survive the world being a black man. Those adversities and/or traumas could or have developed into an outlook of how the world would view us as undesirable or devalued. From discrimination and stereotypes, mental illness and suicide, to cultural norms or systemic inequalities, to understand a black man, one must want to listen to our pain.

No one can understand the pain of a father having to strip away small pieces of innocence from their sons by teaching them the reality of how the world sees them. We can prepare to be proud and unapologetically black men, but on the flip side, you must always protect yourself. Most of the time we understand that we must grow up much faster than our counterparts in many areas. It's easy to call someone angry, but will they try to find out why?

Proverbs 4:23 says, "Above all else, GUARD YOUR HEART." What happens when guarding your heart has turned into closing the world out, being unable to be vulnerable, or not trusting anyone? Why does it feel like everything is expected of me?

1 Corinthians 6:19 says, "Do you not know that your bodies are temples."

One night, I woke up to a thought running through my head. I don't know about you, but I am forced to get up to write when information rushes through my mind while trying to sleep. Otherwise, I'd never be able to go to sleep peacefully. But I digress. "Does an experience change your perception? Does a perception change your mind? Does a changed mind change your feelings? Does changed feelings change behaviour? The simple answer is YES. Do you see how everything is connected? Unloading instead of tucking it away; better yet, forgiving instead of storing. Forgiving is not for them; it is for you". We tend to hold on to way too much until it becomes bigger than we can carry or handle, and that is where the explosions of anger, stress, and depression stem from. The part of forgiveness that most don't mention is learning to forgive yourself. Sometimes, it is in our own doing that we are angry, hurt, or misunderstood.

If there were an equation for unforgiveness, it would probably look like this.

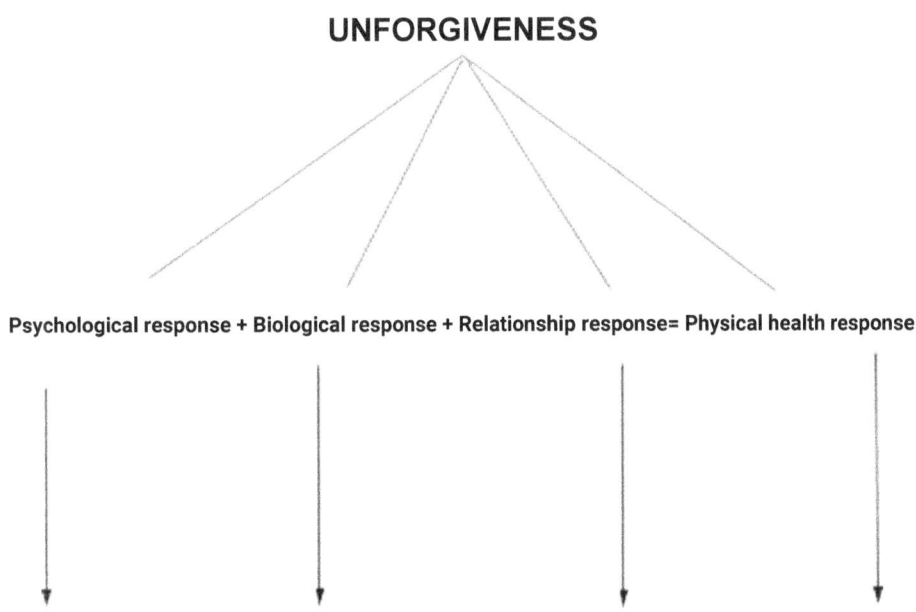

UNFORGIVENESS

Psychological response + Biological response + Relationship response= Physical health response

Depression and anxiety	The body pulls into dysregulation	Breaks down of communication	Increased risk of heart disease and hypertension
Negative emotions	The body is unable to heal, thus causing illness	Creates tension around others	Elevated stress levels
Mental exhaustion	Triggers stress response and staying in survival mode	Distorts view of relationships and connections with others	Increased chance of diabetes and other chronic conditions and mortality rates

If you can spend time mad at yourself for where you are and what you've done, you can be proud of how far you've come and where you are. Take time to enjoy the blessings, and stop always looking for the "MORE."

What does forgiveness look like to you?

Learn to forgive to lose the weight of hurt!!!

Matthew 18: 21-35

SINS OF THE FATHER

Take care of your past so it doesn't bleed into your future.

What does "SINS OF THE FATHER" mean to you?

Most people see the saying "sins of the father" and only relate it to the negative things he has done in the past that the children end up having to deal with in the form of some type of backlash. I want to offer you a different outlook. Let us say that something or multiple things happened to you in your past that you never learned how to deal with or heal from.

I want you to take a second and think about a situation in your life that used to trigger you or still does from something that happened to you. Do you think the feelings that come from just thinking about your past will resurface in the future?

In 2018, I decided to return to school to finish my degree. Unfortunately, I had to leave my son for a few months in Florida while returning to Utah. I wanted to take him with me but wasn't allowed to do that. The interaction with my son changed so much in just those few months of me being gone. After I graduated and returned, I started seeing things in my son that weren't sitting well with me, but didn't understand. There was one situation that happened that opened my eyes to what they were.

One day, my son and I went to see a friend. As we got in the car to leave, the weirdest thing (at the time) happened. I put the car in reverse, and instantly, police sirens sounded off. I'm going into processing mode, trying to recall if I had done anything or if they're about to pick on me. Those thoughts came quicker than my eyes could even realize that there wasn't anything behind me and also quicker than I realized that my 4-year-old son was in the back seat hysterically crying and yelling, saying, "I don't want us to die. I don't want you to go to jail." My first response to hearing him say that was disbelief, which immediately turned into anger. What happened while I was gone? Who hurt him? Was there an interaction with cops that I didn't know about?

I called his mother to get some answers to what was going on. She assures me that there have never been any situations involving cops. I've tried my best to make sure I live a life that he and I can both be proud of. After sitting with this and trying to figure things out, it hit. My past experiences and traumas dealing with police were resurfacing; unfortunately, it was resurfacing in my son.

I've heard about a parent passing things on to their children, but I never thought experiences could be one of those things. That situation opened my eyes to the things I was trying to figure out in what I was seeing in my son that I wasn't comfortable seeing. My feelings of neglect, anxiety, fear, traumas, and a plethora of other things were finally getting answered. My son was the direct embodiment of my feelings and experiences but amplified.

Now that I understand those things, I am aware that we are solely responsible for the weight our children are left carrying. We, as black men, know that we must have tough conversations with our children, sons especially, about the reality of life that you will be hated purely for existing. From dealing with anger, police, racism, everyday systemic issues, and even sex, those are conversations we must have. When is the right time to have those talks? If you have a child of a mixed race, then that's an entirely different conversation in dealing with identity crisis and reality.

Whether you are conscious or unconscious of it, you are tied to the weight and readiness of your child to carry such things. So take care of yourself so you can take care of the ones watching and taking after you. Understanding how to deal with your traumas so you'll know how to deal with them if you see them rise in your seed.

Everyone's so worried about passing on generational wealth while not realizing they're passing on generational hurt.

IS IT A BAD SEED, OR IS IT THE ONE PLANTING IT?

INTERGENERATIONAL TRAUMA

The cycle of trauma passing through generations within a family.

Many of us don't realize the battles we were or are still fighting don't even belong to us, but we have made it our own. I implore you and pray that each person reading this will sit down and evaluate their life, see what in your past may come back up, and take care of it. We have so much pain, hurt, and unresolved traumas from our predecessors that it may take a lifetime to deal with, but as long as we start the process, our future may look better than the present.

Can you think of anything from your past that could come back into your life, either through you or your children?

What are some ways you could deal with them?

OUR STRENGTH IS NOT MEASURED BY HOW MUCH
TRAUMA WEIGHT WE CAN CARRY! UNLOAD THE
HURT SO WE CAN TRAVEL FASTER TO HEALING

(Holding it in and moving forward doesn't make it better; it just
makes it more potent when it comes back up)

A MISSED DREAM

Continuing on the topic of passing things down to our children is the topic of trying to live vicariously through our children. It is one thing to push your child to understand hard work and the importance of pursuing a goal. It's an entirely different thing to push them because you were unable to reach yours, so you are putting it in them. Too many times, parents push their children into things the child may not even want to do ultimately, which ends up putting unnecessary pressure on them, which in turn may cause mental health issues and delay development in other areas of their lives.

Speaking from experience, most of my career was played solely to get my family out of financial hardships. We hear that story way too often. The part we don't hear about is the pressure that comes with that as a kid.

One morning, my dad was taking me and one of my brothers to school, and on the way, he wanted to have a heart-to-heart. The heart-to-heart, unfortunately, came at the expense of our emotional and mental state. I know his intent was not to make us feel bad, but man, did he hurt us. The hurt came in the form of a burden. "Man, listen, y'all have to make it. Y'all have to make it. To get your family out of this mess. I'm tired of struggling. Y'all have to make it." I've always stated that football was a place of peace for me, but in that moment, it became something more. My brother and I went into the school with faces full of tears. On arrival, instead of our regular routine of going to the cafeteria, we went to our separate coaches' offices to have a conversation. At the time, I was a freshman on varsity trying to work my way onto the field. Until this day, I have never begged for an opportunity to prove myself again. The amount of shame I felt, even at that young age, put a horrible taste in my mouth.

As I stated before, I don't believe that was my dad's intent, but he doesn't know how much pressure that put on us. The game was no longer just fun but a job and a responsibility to get the family out of the struggle. I never thought about anything other than being an NFL player, and yes, that goal was knocking at my front door (so to speak). In the process, I never really developed a mindset to see past the game, which stunted my development as a regular human being. Everything was football or track to get better speed for football, so when there was no more football, the feeling of being helpless, unwanted, or just flat-out lost was the first feeling to show its face. I mentioned in my other book, <u>WHEN THE LIGHTS ARE BRIGHTEST: Reinvention of Self</u> <u>after Sports,</u> that the loss of my dream and goal caused me to constantly dream of taking my life because, without football, who was I? What good was I without it? The thought of never being able to get my family out of the struggle, and so many thoughts kept playing in my head.

You hear about other children who aren't so fortunate to still be here due to the pressure put on them by family situations and the weight they will never be able to speak about. We see too often young people leave the sport and revert back to the things they were trying to escape because of the lack of development in life skills.

Having been one of those kids carrying unnecessary weight, there is no way I would ever want to pass that on to my kid. There are so many aspects of sports that are applicable to everyday life, which is why I would want my son to participate, but to force something on him to live out my failed dream or goal would be wrong of me. I do introduce sports to him to learn, but I also know he is more of the artsy type. I would be lying if I said it didn't bother me at first, but when I realize the struggle I went through with just knowing who I was without a game, there is no way I would put that burden on him.

It's already hard enough having to grow up too fast just for being born black. We shouldn't add more to our children's plates than we wouldn't want. Sit back for a minute and think about how tough your parents were on you for dropping a pass, missing a shot, or not winning a race. The feeling of being a failure, never being able to fulfill your parents' expectations, resentment because you needed a parent for support and not a coach, frustration, neglect, or flat out having to be the family's way out. As black men, we already know the weight of carrying things as adults and the effects it has on our mental, physical, spiritual, and emotional well-being. We know the feeling of being looked at solely for what we can do, not who we are. We know it is tough to pave our way when everyone is telling us who to be, how to be it, and when to be it. We understand the feeling of not having the support from the ones we thought would give it to us.

WHY WOULD WE WANT
OUR CHILDREN TO GO THROUGH THAT?

I know we all want what is best for our children, but if I could offer just a bit of advice. Allow them to show you who they are and cultivate that.

THINGS TO TRY

- **Self Reflect**

  Why are you pushing your dream on your child?

  Do they want this?

- **Identify Dreams and Goals**

  What dreams did you have for yourself?

  What dreams do they have for themselves?

  How do they align?

- **Encourage and Explore**

  What are their interests?

- **Listen**

  Have a conversation about what they want and/or like, which could open the door to allow you to explain the positives from your old dream.

- **Acknowledge**

  Celebrate successes and failures as long as they learn from it.

- **Void Pressure**

  They are not you, so let go of that idea.

- **Focus on Growth**

  How are they developing?

  What habits have they formed?

  Are they learning from their failed attempts?

- **Balance**

  Understand when to push and when to back off.

- **Encourage Independence**

  Allow them to figure things out on their own and let them make some decisions. (within reason)

- **Be Their Fan and Biggest Supporter**

21 QUESTIONS

I'm sure there are thousands of questions one could ask themselves or others on improving themselves, but here are 21 questions on self-reflection, career/finance community, personal growth, relationships, legacy, and improvement.

1. WHO AM I? (without listing your accolades/ acknowledgements/career)

2. What have I done in the past that has slowed my progress, and how can I do better?

3. What personal values would I want to demonstrate and embody in my daily life?

4. How can I prioritize my overall physical and mental health?

5. What do I need to acquire to reach my goal?

6. How can I develop and grow meaningful relationships?

7. What mindset should I challenge within myself that is limiting my development?

8. How can I better manage stress and practice self-care?

9. To broaden my views, what new experiences or perspectives could I seek?

10. How could I improve communication to foster healthier relationships?

11. How can I create a stronger support system for myself?

12. How could I be more supportive of those around me?

13. What legacy do I want to leave behind

14. How could I help the black community break stereotypes that limit us?

15. What groups or causes align with my views and morals that would make me want to join their cause?

16. How can I better my financial literacy and build wealth?

17. What steps can I take to advance my career or pursue my passions?

18. How can I be a positive role model in my community?

19. How can I use my voice and presence to address issues affecting the black community?

20. What habits can I develop to improve the chance of success in personal and professional growth?

21. How do I assess my progress and success while adjusting my goals?

MINDFUL
REFLECTIONS

CREATING PROGRAM/COMMUNITY

CREATE A MISSION/ VISION: DEFINE THE PURPOSE

- Provide a space for black men to connect, share, and support each other

- Promote mental health awareness and well-being

- Offer mentorships and professional development opportunities

- Community Outreach

COMPONENTS OF THE PROGRAM

MENTAL HEALTH SUPPORT

- Partner with other organizations that would offer therapy and other mental health services

- Schedule regular group discussions on various topics

- Offer resources and education to break the negative narrative on mental health

PROFESSIONAL DEVELOPMENT

- Networking events

- Skills workshops

- Resume and interview preparation assistance

COMMUNITY SERVICES

Give back to the community

- Volunteer opportunity

- Partner with local organizations for different projects

- Encourage members to become mentors themselves.

STRATEGIES

- Online platforms

- Regular meetups

- Partnerships

- Content creation

- Leadership structure

- Funding

PLAN

- Research

- Small group to start

- Marketing and Outreach

- Evaluation and feedback (make necessary changes)

You can significantly impact black men and the black community by creating a supportive community for Black men. Everything starts with us and could very well end with us. Let us create a new normal!

Continue to shape your mind as you continue to shape your child's.

In my other book, When the Lights Are Brightest, Reinvention of Self after Sports, I listed seven steps helping one figure out who they are. Feel your feelings, get help, know yourself, eliminate negative emotions, create good habits and community, know your why, stay active, and be patient. Those same seven steps can be applied to this as well.

What is a man to you?

What is a man's role?

Most of us may have difficulty answering the last one because we often attach what we do to who we are. I believe that to answer that question, you have to be able to answer other relatively simple but complex questions.

Additional questions to ask yourself:

- What do I like and/or hate?

- What are my strengths and/or weaknesses?

- What makes me happy?

- What is happiness to you?

- What makes me different?

- What are my beliefs?

- Do I understand my feelings?

Each of us has a calling on our lives. We must not look only at what's in front of us, but look at, walk in, and focus on our purpose. If you do not walk in your purpose, you will end up medicating in pleasure.

Momentary pleasures do not solve current or future problems.

GOD HAS GIVEN US THE INGREDIENTS; IT IS OUR JOB TO PUT THEM TOGETHER TO FORM WHAT IS MEANT FOR US TO BE

TAP IN

Now that you have finished the book, I want you to try something out. I'd like for you to close your eyes and try to separate yourself into three individuals. Those three individuals are a son, a black man, and a father (if you are one).

I want you to reflect on what feelings or thoughts were evoked as you made your way through the book.

Each one should be answered individually.

There is no right or wrong answer!
There's only you
If you'd like to share your responses, scan the QR code

Or email me at
dbrunson14@gmail.com